Speak Intelligent

Gaining Knowledge of Business Communication for Success

By

Ramiro Wilson

Disclaimer

Copyright © by Ramiro Wilson 2024. All rights reserved.

Before this document is duplicated or reproduced in any manner, the publisher's consent must be gained.

Therefore, the contents within can neither be stored electronically, transferred, nor kept in a database. Neither in part nor in full can the document be copied, scanned, faxed, or retained without approval from the publisher or creator.

Table of Content

INTRODUCTION — 6

WELCOME TO SPEAK INTELLIGENCE. — 6
THE POWER OF STRATEGIC COMMUNICATION — 7

CHAPTER 1: THE ART OF INTELLIGENT MESSAGING. — 11

CRAFTING CLEAR AND STRATEGIC MESSAGES — 11
MASTERING TONE AND VOICE — 14
TAILORING COMMUNICATION FOR DIFFERENT AUDIENCES — 16

CHAPTER 2: STRATEGIC LISTENING FOR SUCCESS. — 21

THE ART OF ACTIVE LISTENING. — 21
EMPATHETIC LISTENING IN BUSINESS — 23
LEVERAGING LISTENING TO BUILD RELATIONSHIPS — 25

CHAPTER 3: NONVERBAL INTELLIGENCE: LANGUAGE BEYOND WORDS — 29

UNDERSTANDING BODY LANGUAGE IN BUSINESS. — 29
INTERPRETING FACIAL EXPRESSIONS AND GESTURES — 32
USING NONVERBAL CUES FOR EFFECTIVE COMMUNICATION — 35

CHAPTER 4: STRATEGIC WRITING: CREATING PERSUASIVE BUSINESS DOCUMENT — 39

WRITING PROFESSIONAL EMAILS AND MEMOS. — 39

Creating impactful reports and proposals 42
Enhancing Written Communication for Success 44

CHAPTER 5: THE POWER OF PERSUASION: HOW TO INFLUENCE OTHERS WITH INTEGRITY 49

Understanding the principles of persuasion. 49
Applying the Psychology of Influence 52
Practical Strategies for Persuasion 54
Ethical Considerations for Persuasion 55

CHAPTER 6: STRATEGIC MEETINGS: MAXIMUM IMPACT 59

Planning and Leading Strategic Meetings 60
Engaging participants and facilitating productive discussions. 62
Strategies for Following Up and Action Planning 65

CHAPTER 7: STRATEGIC PRESENTATIONS FOR CAPTIVATING AUDIENCES 69

Creating Engaging and Persuasive Presentations 70
Deliver with Confidence and Authority 72
Enhancing Visual Aids for Maximum Impact. 74

CHAPTER 8: STRATEGIC NETWORKING: ESTABLISHING MEANINGFUL CONNECTIONS 79

Developing and nurturing professional relationships 80
Leveraging Networking Events and Platforms 82
Building a Strategic Network for Success. 85

CHAPTER 9: CULTURAL INTELLIGENCE AND BUSINESS COMMUNICATION — 89

Understanding Cultural Differences in Communication — 90
Adapting Communication Styles across Cultures — 92
Developing Cross-cultural Competence for Success — 95

CHAPTER 10: STRATEGIC FEEDBACK AND RECOGNITION. — 99

Giving and Receiving Feedback Effectively — 100
Recognizing and Acknowledging Contributions — 102
Promoting a Culture of Growth and Appreciation — 105

CONCLUSION: REFLECTING ON YOUR PATH TO COMMUNICATION MASTERY — 109

Reflecting on Your Journey. — 109
Moving Forward with Confidence and Purpose. — 110

Introduction

Welcome to Speak Intelligence.

Welcome, fellow traveler, to the world of strategic communication, where every word carries the weight of possibility and every interaction presents an opportunity for influence and inspiration. In this first chapter of "Speak Intelligent: Gaining Knowledge of Business Communication for Success," we'll go on a trip together that will change the way you think, communicate, and interact in the dynamic world of business.

Consider the following scenario: you are on the verge of launching a new business, armed with vision, expertise, and ambition. However, as you survey the landscape before you, you understand that success is determined not just by what you know, but also by how well you can communicate that knowledge to others. Welcome to the power of strategic communication—a force with the potential to change destiny, build alliances, and propel you to new heights of success.

But what is strategic communication, and why is it so important in today's business landscape? Strategic communication is more than just sending information; it is about constructing communications with intent, forethought, and precision to achieve specified goals. Whether you're selling a fresh idea to investors, negotiating a contract with clients, or leading a team toward a single objective, strategic communication is the glue that ties everything together.

In the following pages, we will look at the multifaceted nature of strategic communication in the business world, unraveling its mysteries and secrets. But, before we get into the practical methods and procedures that will enable you to communicate with intelligence and refinement, let's take time to consider the significance of this trip and the transforming influence it may have on your personal and professional lives.

The Power of Strategic Communication

In today's fast-paced and hyper-connected world, effective communication is not simply a desired ability; it is a requirement. From boardrooms to break rooms, virtual meetings to social media platforms, effective communication has become the currency of success in many aspects of business and beyond.

Consider the importance of strategic communication in a high-stakes negotiation. As you sit across the table from your counterparts, every word you say has the potential to sway opinions, build trust, and ultimately secure a positive outcome. Strategic communication allows you to confidently negotiate the complexities of the negotiating process, using language to alter views and achieve your goals.

Strategic communication, however, has far-reaching implications beyond negotiations and deal-making. Strategic communication is essential for success in all aspects of business, from marketing and sales to leadership and teamwork. It allows you to communicate your ideas clearly and convincingly, connect with your audience on a deeper level, inspire action, and generate results.

However, despite its importance, strategic communication is frequently misunderstood and devalued. Many people wrongly believe that good communication is just speaking clearly and confidently, unaware of the skill's depth and complexity. But do not worry, dear reader, because "Speak Intelligent" is here to demystify the art of strategic communication and provide you with the knowledge and tools you need to succeed in any corporate environment.

As we progress through the chapters, we will cover a wide range of topics, including drafting clear and engaging messages, learning the nuances of nonverbal communication, navigating conflict with delicacy, and building lasting relationships through networking. Each chapter will include practical ideas, real-world examples, and concrete tactics to help you communicate intelligently, empathically, and effectively.

So, dear reader, I ask you to accompany me on this revolutionary journey—one that will not only improve your professional performance but also enrich your relationships and improve your general quality of life. Let us work together to unlock the power of strategic communication and realize our full potential as corporate leaders, innovators, and change-makers. Welcome to "Speak Intelligent," where every word can change lives, form alliances, and propel success.

Chapter 1: The Art of Intelligent Messaging.

Welcome to Chapter One of "Speak Intelligent: Gaining Knowledge of Business Communication for Success." In this chapter, we look at the foundation of effective communication: the art of intelligent messages. In this section, we'll look at how to create clear, strategic messages that connect with your audience, motivate action, and achieve your goals. Practical ideas, real-world examples, and actionable tactics will teach you how to use your words to communicate intelligently, emphatically, and effectively.

Crafting Clear and Strategic Messages

Effective communication begins with creating clear and targeted messages that cut through the noise and attract your audience's attention. Whether you're giving a presentation, writing an email, or having a one-on-one chat, the ability to communicate your ideas clearly and precisely is essential.

But what precisely does it mean to create clear, strategic messages? At its foundation, effective messaging requires condensing complicated ideas into basic, digestible concepts that are easy for your audience to understand. It asks you to eliminate jargon, prevent ambiguity, and go right to the point. Strategic messaging, on the other hand, goes beyond basic clarity; it entails adapting your message to achieve certain goals, such as persuading others to take action, establishing rapport and trust, or communicating empathy and understanding.

To create clear and strategic messaging, begin by establishing your objectives. What are you hoping to achieve through your communication? Do you want to inform, convince, inspire, or educate? Once your objectives are clear, customize your message accordingly, using the most relevant language, tone, and delivery style to achieve your desired result.

Assume you're pitching a new product to potential investors. Your goal is to persuade them to invest in your venture and share your vision. When designing your message, you may want to emphasize your product's distinctive features and benefits, demonstrate its market potential, and articulate a compelling value proposition that speaks to your target audience's requirements and interests.

Consider your audience's wants and preferences while crafting your message. What are their pain issues, difficulties, and goals? How can your messaging give value while also addressing their concerns? Understanding your audience's perspective allows you to personalize your message to their interests and priorities, improving the likelihood of a positive response.

Effective message demands not only clarity and strategic relevance but also honesty and sincerity. People can see whether a message is false or manipulative, so speak with honesty, integrity, and transparency. Authenticity fosters trust and credibility, resulting in deeper connections and greater relationships with your audience.

Mastering Tone and Voice

In addition to crafting clear and strategic ideas, controlling tone and voice is critical to effective communication. Your tone and voice express not only the content of your communication, but also your attitude, personality, and emotional condition. Mastering tone and voice allows you to portray confidence, warmth, empathy, and authority, increasing the impact of your message and developing relationships with your audience.

Tone describes the emotional character of your communication—how you portray your attitude, mood, and sentiments via your words and delivery. It includes pitch, tempo, volume, and intonation, as well as nonverbal indicators including facial expressions, gestures, and body language. For example, a warm and enthusiastic tone may be ideal for giving good news or expressing gratitude, but a calm and reassuring tone may be more appropriate for addressing worries or resolving disputes.

In contrast, voice refers to your distinct style and personality as a communicator—the way you express yourself through word choice, phrasing, and syntax. Your voice reflects your values, views, and worldview, which influence how people interpret and respond to your message. For example, a confident and aggressive voice may be beneficial for delivering a persuasive argument or making a big statement, whereas a conversational and approachable voice may be more engaging for establishing rapport and promoting collaboration.

To master tone and voice, first, identify your natural communication style and strengths. Are you naturally extroverted and expressive, or are you more quiet and introverted? Do you like a formal and professional tone, or are you more at ease with a casual and conversational approach? Understanding your communication abilities and preferences allows you to customize your tone and voice to your audience's requirements and expectations.

Next, practice changing your tone and voice to fit different contexts and situations. For example, in a formal business context, you may need to use a more professional and authoritative tone, yet in a casual social setting, you may use a more relaxed and informal tone. Pay attention to your audience's reactions and comments, and modify your tone and voice accordingly to keep them engaged and connected.

Finally, when you communicate with people, develop your self-awareness and empathy skills. Consider how your audience will perceive your tone and voice. Are you coming off as sincere and authentic, or are you accidentally sending a negative or off-putting message? By building empathy and understanding, you can establish trust and rapport with your audience, resulting in a positive and effective communication environment.

Tailoring Communication for Different Audiences

One of the distinguishing features of effective communication is the ability to adjust your message to the needs and tastes of various audiences. Whether you're speaking to a group of coworkers, addressing a client, or interacting with a possible investor, you must adjust your communication style, tone, and substance to connect with your audience and achieve your goal.

To personalize your communication with diverse audiences, first learn their background, interests, and communication preferences. Do they understand your industry and language, or do they require more context and explanation? What are their objectives, issues, and priorities, and how can your message offer value and meet their requirements? By taking the time to understand your audience's point of view, you can create a message that addresses their specific interests and problems, boosting the likelihood of a positive response.

Next, think about the cultural and social framework in which your audience functions. Are there any cultural conventions, taboos, or sensitivities you should be aware of? How does their cultural background affect their communication style and preferences? Acknowledging and appreciating cultural differences allows you to prevent misunderstandings and establish deeper connections with your audience, ultimately building trust and confidence.

In addition to understanding your audience's background and cultural context, customize your message to meet their communication preferences and expectations. Some audiences may prefer a formal and professional tone, whereas others may prefer a more relaxed and conversational approach. Similarly, some audiences may prefer written communication, such as emails or reports, but others may prefer verbal communication, such as in-person meetings or speeches. By tailoring your communication style, tone, and format to your audience's preferences, you may boost the impact of your message and the likelihood of a favorable outcome.

Finally, think about the precise aims and goals for your communication. What do you want to accomplish by communicating your message to this specific audience? Do you want to inform, convince, inspire, or educate? Clarifying your objectives and aligning your message will guarantee that your communication resonates with your audience and leads to the intended action or response.

To summarize, creating clear and strategic messaging entails tailoring your communication to your audience's requirements and preferences, adjusting your tone and voice to show authenticity and sincerity, and aligning your message with your aims and goals.

Mastering the art of intelligent messaging allows you to communicate with intelligence, empathy, and impact, resulting in increased trust, credibility, and rapport with your audience and success in any corporate context.

Verdict

In this chapter, we looked at intelligent messaging, which is the foundation of good business communication. We've learned how to create clear and smart communications that connect with our audience, inspire action, and achieve our goals. We've perfected tone and voice, knowing how to convey honesty, sincerity, and empathy through our communication. And we've adapted our communication to different audiences' requirements, tastes, and expectations.

As you continue your journey through "Speak Intelligent: Gaining Knowledge of Business Communication for Success," keep in mind that mastering the art of intelligent communicating is a continuous process that involves practice, patience, and perseverance. By following the ideas and tactics discussed in this chapter, you may communicate with intelligence, empathy, and impact, establishing trust, credibility, and rapport with your audience and achieving success in any business setting. So, dear reader, I encourage you to embrace the power of intelligent messaging and reach your full communicative potential. The world is waiting for your message; speak with intelligence and watch as doors of opportunity open wide before you.

Chapter 2: Strategic Listening for Success.

Welcome to Chapter Two of "Speak Intelligent: Gaining Knowledge of Business Communication for Success." In this chapter, we'll look at the transforming impact of strategic listening—a talent that's often overlooked yet necessary for effective communication in the business world. Here, we'll look at active listening, sympathetic listening, and how to use listening to establish connections, foster collaboration, and achieve success. Through practical insights, real-world examples, and actionable tactics, you will discover how to become a strategic listener and maximize your communication abilities.

The Art of Active Listening.

Active listening is more than just hearing; it is about fully engaging with the speaker, understanding their point of view, and responding with empathy, respect, and understanding. Active listening, as opposed to passive listening, demands intention, focus, and presence.

So, what does it mean to be an engaged listener? It includes several crucial components:

1. Pay attention to the speaker's words, tone, and body language. Minimize distractions and refrain from interrupting or multitasking while they speak.

2. Show Interest: Show genuine interest in what the speaker is saying by nodding, making eye contact, and utilizing verbal and nonverbal clues to indicate your engagement and attention.

3. Provide Feedback: To indicate understanding, provide feedback and validation to the speaker by paraphrasing their words, asking clarifying questions, and reflecting on their emotions.

4. Empathize: Try to grasp the speaker's perspective, feelings, and motivations. Show empathy and compassion by acknowledging and valuing their feelings and experiences.

5. Defer Judgment: Postpone judgment and avoid leaping to conclusions or providing unwanted counsel. Listen with an open mind, allowing the speaker to freely express oneself without fear of criticism or judgment.

Active listening can help you build a supportive and sympathetic communication environment, resulting in deeper connections and stronger relationships with colleagues, clients, and stakeholders. Active listening improves your comprehension of difficult topics, allowing you to make better decisions and respond more effectively to the needs and concerns of others.

Empathetic Listening in Business

In addition to active listening, empathic listening is essential for effective corporate communication. Empathetic listening entails not just comprehending the speaker's words, but also their emotions, sentiments, underlying needs, and concerns. It demands you to put yourself in the speaker's shoes, attempting to view the world through their eyes and responding with empathy and compassion.

Empathetic listening is especially useful in situations involving strong emotions, such as disagreements, negotiations, or tough conversations. Empathic listening allows you to acknowledge the speaker's feelings and experiences, reduce tension, and create a secure space for open and honest discussion. This, in turn, promotes trust, respect, and mutual understanding, laying the groundwork for resolution and reconciliation.

To practice empathic listening, first acknowledge the speaker's feelings and validate their experiences. Use comments like "I can see you're frustrated" or "It sounds like you're very passionate about this issue" to demonstrate empathy and understanding. Even if you disagree with their point of view, you should not minimize or disregard their feelings.

Next, paraphrase the speaker's words and reflect on their emotions to exhibit understanding. For example, you may say, "It sounds like you're feeling overwhelmed by the workload" or "You appear to be concerned about meeting the deadline." This demonstrates that you're listening carefully and taking their worries seriously.

Finally, respond with respect and compassion, providing support and reassurance as needed. Validate the speaker's experiences and sentiments, even if you don't always agree with them. By demonstrating empathy and compassion, you may establish trust and rapport with your colleagues, clients, and stakeholders, resulting in a pleasant and supportive communication environment in which everyone feels valued and appreciated.

Leveraging Listening to Build Relationships

Strategic listening is important not only in individual encounters but also in developing connections and encouraging collaboration in the workplace. Listening attentively and empathetically to your colleagues, clients, and stakeholders can help you create connections, build trust, and foster an open communication and collaboration culture.

In team settings, for example, strategic listening allows you to foster a supportive and inclusive environment in which everyone feels heard and respected. By actively listening to team members' ideas, concerns, and feedback, you may promote creativity, innovation, and problem-solving, resulting in better outcomes and enhanced team cohesion.

Similarly, strategic listening in client interactions allows you to establish trust and rapport by exhibiting empathy, comprehension, and responsiveness to their wants and concerns. By carefully listening to your client's goals, issues, and priorities, you can personalize your solutions and services to their requirements, enhancing client happiness and loyalty.

To use listening to establish connections, begin by fostering open and honest conversations with your coworkers, clients, and stakeholders. Encourage children to express their ideas, concerns, and feedback freely, without fear of being judged or punished. Actively listen to their viewpoints, validate their experiences, and respond with respect and compassion.

Next, demonstrate responsiveness by acting on feedback and concerns from colleagues, clients, and stakeholders. Whether you're introducing new policies and procedures, resolving issues and challenges, or recognizing and appreciating contributions, demonstrate that you're listening and taking their concerns seriously.

Finally, foster an appreciation and recognition culture by honoring the accomplishments and contributions of your colleagues, clients, and stakeholders. Recognizing their efforts and accomplishments can help you build relationships, increase morale, and develop a sense of belonging and loyalty inside your firm.

Verdict

In this chapter, we looked at the transforming potential of strategic listening, a talent that is required for effective communication in business. We've learned how to listen actively, and empathetically, and use listening as a tool to establish relationships, foster collaboration, and achieve success. By learning the skill of strategic listening, you can foster a good and supportive communication climate in which everyone feels heard, valued, and respected. So, dear reader, I invite you to embrace the power of strategic listening and maximize the effectiveness of your communication skills. The world is waiting for your message; listen strategically and watch as doors of opportunity open wide before you.

Chapter 3: Nonverbal Intelligence: Language beyond Words

Welcome to Chapter Three of "Speak Intelligent: Gaining Knowledge of Business Communication for Success." In this chapter, we will look at the intriguing world of nonverbal communication—a language that says volumes without words. Here, we delve into the complexities of body language, facial expressions, and gestures, revealing the keys to deciphering nonverbal signs and employing them to improve communication efficacy. Through practical insights, real-world examples, and concrete methods, you will discover how to use nonverbal intelligence to develop trust, convey confidence, and influence others in the workplace.

Understanding Body Language in Business.

Body language is a powerful kind of nonverbal communication that may reveal a lot about a person's thoughts, emotions, and intentions. Our body language conveys subtle signals that others intuitively understand, often without conscious awareness.

Understanding and interpreting body language is critical in business for developing rapport, establishing trust, and communicating confidence and reliability. Whether you're giving a presentation, negotiating a sale, or attending a meeting, your body language can either support or undercut the message you're attempting to portray.

So, what are some important characteristics of body language to be mindful of in business settings? Here are a few.

1. Posture: Your posture conveys a great deal about your confidence and professionalism. Standing or sitting up straight exudes confidence and authority, yet slouching or hunching over can make you appear disinterested or disengaged. Pay attention to your posture and make modifications as needed to project a positive and confident image.

2. Gestures can help your vocal communication become more engaging and

remembered. However, gestures should be used rarely and purposefully, as they can detract from your message. When making gestures, make sure they are natural and consistent with your words, and avoid movements that could be interpreted as hostile or insulting.

3. Eye Contact: Eye contact is a powerful nonverbal communication tool that indicates trust, confidence, and involvement. Maintaining good eye contact demonstrates that you are interested and attentive, but avoiding eye contact makes you appear untrustworthy or uneasy. When interacting with people, keep eye contact but avoid staring or making others feel uncomfortable.

4. Facial Expressions: Your facial expressions can tell a lot about your feelings and intentions. Smiling indicates warmth and friendliness, whereas frowning or scowling may indicate dislike or disapproval. Pay attention to your facial expressions and make an effort to remain nice and approachable, even in difficult times.

5. Space and Proximity: Your closeness to others can reveal a lot about your connection and degree of comfort. Invading someone's personal space might come across as pushy or intrusive, yet standing too far away can make you appear distant or disinterested. Pay attention to social conventions and cues, and change your proximity accordingly, to ensure a pleasant and courteous connection.

Understanding and mastering the nuances of body language will help you improve your communication skills and develop deeper relationships with your coworkers, clients, and stakeholders. Pay attention to your own and others' body language, and utilize it to show confidence, credibility, and trustworthiness in all professional encounters.

Interpreting facial expressions and Gestures

Facial expressions and gestures are effective ways to convey emotions, intentions, and attitudes in communication. Nonverbal cues, such as a warm smile or a strong handshake, can have a long-term impact on others and alter how they perceive and respond to your message.

In the professional sector, learning the art of analyzing facial expressions and gestures is critical for developing rapport, establishing trust, and communicating empathy and understanding. Whether you're meeting with clients, negotiating with stakeholders, or managing a team, understanding and interpreting nonverbal signs can provide you with vital insights into the thoughts, feelings, and intentions of others.

So, what are some frequent facial expressions and gestures to be aware of in the workplace? Here are a few.

1. Smiling: A genuine grin demonstrates warmth, friendliness, and approachability. It might help to put others at ease and foster a good and welcoming environment.

2. Maintaining good eye contact indicates that you are interested and attentive. It demonstrates confidence, honesty, and participation, which aids in the establishment of rapport and trust.

3. Handshake: A firm handshake is a traditional business greeting that conveys confidence, professionalism, and respect. A limp or weak handshake may be viewed as unassertive or fake, therefore shake hands firmly and decisively.

4. Nodding: A nonverbal indication that indicates agreement, comprehension, or encouragement. It might demonstrate that you are actively listening and participating in the conversation, even if you are not speaking.

5. Mirroring is the activity of subtly mirroring the body language of someone you're engaging with. It can help you establish rapport and a sense of connection with others.

6. Open vs. Closed Body Language: Leaning forward, facing the person you're conversing with, and keeping your arms uncrossed communicate openness, receptivity, and interest. Closed body language, such as crossing your arms, looking away, or avoiding eye contact, might indicate defensiveness, apathy, or disagreement.

Paying attention to facial expressions and gestures and learning to analyze their meanings can provide vital insights into other people's thoughts, feelings, and intentions. This, in turn, can help you strengthen relationships, communicate more effectively, and achieve greater results in business dealings.

Using Nonverbal Cues for Effective Communication

In addition to knowing and interpreting nonverbal cues, learning how to use them for effective communication is critical for business success. By employing nonverbal cues consciously and strategically, you may improve your communication efficacy, establish trust and rapport with people, and positively affect their views and behavior.

So, how do you use nonverbal clues to improve your communication effectiveness? Here are some strategies to consider:

1. Be Aware of Your Body Language: Begin by becoming aware of your body language and any nonverbal indications you are providing to

others. Pay attention to your posture, gestures, facial expressions, and tone of voice, and make any necessary adjustments to show confidence, warmth, and professionalism.

2. Use Nonverbal Cues to Reinforce Your Message: Nonverbal cues can help to strengthen and underline your verbal message, making it more engaging and memorable. For example, utilizing gestures to emphasize crucial ideas, maintaining good eye contact to demonstrate sincerity and confidence, and nodding or smiling to express agreement and encouragement can all assist in improving your communication efficacy.

3. Match Your Nonverbal Clues to Your Audience: When employing nonverbal clues, take into account your audience's preferences and expectations. For example, in certain cultures, direct eye contact is regarded as a sign of respect and engagement, whilst in others it is regarded as hostile or confrontational. By tailoring your nonverbal clues to the cultural norms and preferences of your audience, you can build

Trust and rapport are built more successfully.

4. Pay Attention to Nonverbal Indicators from Others: In addition to being aware of your nonverbal indicators, take note of the nonverbal signs of others. Observe their body language, facial expressions, and tone of speech to determine their thoughts, feelings, and intentions. This, in turn, can help you answer more effectively and modify your communication style to better fit their requirements.

5. Empathy and emotional intelligence are necessary qualities for effectively utilizing nonverbal signs in conversation. Putting yourself in the shoes of others and understanding their point of view can allow you to better comprehend their nonverbal clues and respond with empathy, understanding, and respect.

By leveraging the power of nonverbal clues, you may improve your communication efficacy, create trust and rapport with others, and achieve greater results in business encounters. Whether you're presenting a presentation, negotiating a sale, or managing a team, mastering nonverbal communication is critical for success in today's dynamic and competitive business environment.

Verdict

In this chapter, we've looked at the intriguing world of nonverbal communication—a language that conveys volumes without words. We've studied how to comprehend and interpret body language, facial emotions, and gestures, as well as how to use nonverbal indicators to improve our communication skills. Mastering the skill of nonverbal intelligence allows us to develop trust, convey confidence, and positively influence people, paving the road for success in business and beyond. So, dear reader, I invite you to embrace the power of nonverbal communication and maximize the effectiveness of your communication skills. The world is waiting for your message; speak with wisdom, empathy, and impact, and watch as opportunities open up in front of you.

Chapter 4: Strategic Writing: Creating Persuasive Business Document

Welcome to Chapter Four of "Speak Intelligent: Gaining Knowledge of Business Communication for Success." In this chapter, we'll look at strategic writing, which is a vital ability for business success. Here, we'll look at how to create convincing business papers including emails, memoranda, reports, and proposals that effectively express your message, impact your audience, and achieve your objectives. Practical insights, real-world examples, and concrete tactics will teach you how to use strategic writing to communicate with clarity, impact, and professionalism.

Writing Professional Emails and Memos.

In today's fast-paced business climate, email and memoranda are common modes of communication, used to deliver information, coordinate activities, and facilitate collaboration among colleagues, clients, and stakeholders. As a result, mastering the art of producing professional emails and memos is critical for success in the modern workplace.

So, what are the main concepts to remember while writing professional emails and memos? Here are a few.

1. Be Clear and Concise: Get right to the point and communicate your message clearly and concisely. Avoid using jargon, convoluted language, or ambiguous claims that may confuse or mislead your readers. Instead, use straightforward language that is easy to read and consume.

2. Maintain a Professional Tone: Regardless of the receiver or topic matter, your emails and memos should have a professional and respectful tone. Address the recipient politely, use appropriate salutations and sign-offs, and avoid slang or informal language that could be viewed as unprofessional.

3. Organize Your Content Effectively: To make your emails and memos easier to read, use

clear headers, subheadings, and bullet points. Use formatting elements like bold, italics, and underlining to emphasize crucial information and critical ideas.

4. When writing emails and memos, keep your audience's requirements, preferences, and expectations in mind. Tailor your message to them. Customize your message to the recipient's role, level of experience, and relationship with you, and use language and tone that they understand.

5. Proofread and edit carefully: Before sending your email or note, be sure it is clear, accurate, and professionally written. Check for spelling and grammatical problems, inappropriate wording, and tone or style inconsistencies, and make the necessary changes.

By adhering to these guidelines, you may create professional emails and memos that successfully convey your message, portray a positive image of yourself and your organization, and promote productive communication and collaboration with your coworkers, clients, and stakeholders.

Creating impactful reports and proposals

Reports and proposals are critical tools for sharing information, presenting conclusions, and making suggestions in business. Whether you're producing a project report for internal stakeholders, a company proposal for possible investors, or a research article for publication, mastering the art of crafting impactful reports and proposals is critical to success.

So, what are some important ideas to bear in mind when producing reports and proposals? Here are a few.

1. Define Your Objectives: Determine the purpose and objectives of your report or proposal ahead of time, and use them as a foundation for organizing and structuring your paper. Clearly state the problem or issue you're addressing, the objectives you expect to achieve, and the important messages you want to express to your audience.

2. Gather and Present Data Effectively: Gather relevant data, evidence, and supporting materials to back up your arguments and recommendations. Present your findings in a clear, structured, and visually appealing format, incorporating tables, charts, graphs, and other visual aids to improve clarity and comprehension.

3. Provide Context and Background: Help your audience comprehend the significance of your report or proposal and how it relates to their needs and interests. Briefly describe the existing situation, including any relevant history or background, and explain why your proposals are significant and necessary.

4. Provide concrete recommendations and actionable insights based on your findings and research. Clearly define the procedures required to address the problem or issue at hand, and provide detailed direction on how to properly implement your recommendations.

5. Anticipate Questions and Objections: Plan ahead of time to address any questions, concerns, or objections that your audience may have concerning your report or plan.

Recognize potential challenges or constraints, and present facts and rationale to back up your judgments and recommendations.

By adhering to these principles, you may create reports and proposals that successfully communicate your message, persuade your audience, and motivate action and decision-making in the workplace.

Enhancing Written Communication for Success

In addition to emails, memos, reports, and proposals, written communication in business can take many different forms, such as letters, presentations, blogs, articles, and social media posts. Regardless of format or media, mastering written communication is critical for success in today's business.

So, what are some effective ways to improve written communication for success? Here are a few.

1. Know Your Audience: Customize your written message to meet the needs,

preferences, and expectations of your target audience. Consider their degree of knowledge, familiarity with the subject, and communication preferences, and use language and tone that speak to them.

2. Be Clear and Concise: Get right to the point and communicate your message clearly and concisely. Avoid using needless phrases, jargon, or technical terms that could confuse or alienate your readers. Instead, use straightforward language that is easy to read and consume.

3. Use Plain Language: Use clear language that is accessible and inclusive to all members of your audience.

, regardless of their background or experience. Avoid using industry-specific language or acronyms without context or explanation, and describe any technical terms or concepts that your audience may not understand.

4. Tell a Compelling Story: Use storytelling tactics to engage your audience and make your written communication more memorable and effective. Frame your message as a narrative

with a distinct beginning, middle, and end, and utilize anecdotes, examples, and case studies to demonstrate and bring your points to life.

5. Edit and Proofread Carefully: Before sending or publishing your written communication, be sure it is clear, accurate, and professional. Check for spelling and grammatical problems, inappropriate wording, and tone or style inconsistencies, and make the necessary changes.

Following these tactics can help you improve your written communication abilities, successfully deliver your message, impact your audience, and achieve your business goals.

Verdict

In this chapter, we looked at the art of strategic writing, which is an essential ability for business success. We've learned how to write effective emails and memos, reports and proposals, and improve written communication for success. Mastering the skill of strategic writing allows you to effectively communicate your message, influence your audience, and achieve your goals in any corporate context. So, dear reader, I invite you to embrace the power of strategic writing and maximize the effectiveness of your communication skills. The world is waiting for your message; speak with knowledge, clarity, and impact, and watch as opportunities open up in front of you.

Chapter 5: The Power of Persuasion: How to Influence Others with Integrity

Welcome to Chapter Five of "Speak Intelligent: Gaining Knowledge of Business Communication for Success." In this chapter, we'll look at the art of persuasion, which is vital for success in business and beyond. We'll look at the concepts of persuasion, the psychology of influence, and practical tactics for convincing others while remaining honest. Through practical insights, real-world examples, and concrete methods, you will learn how to use persuasion to generate agreement, drive change, and achieve your objectives in any corporate setting.

Understanding the principles of persuasion.

Persuasion is fundamentally about convincing people to embrace your point of view, accept your advice, or follow a specific course of action. Whether you're negotiating a sale, selling a product, or managing a team, the ability to persuade others is critical for attaining your objectives and driving success in business.

So, what are some crucial persuasive principles to bear in mind? Here are a few.

1. Reciprocity: According to the concept of reciprocity, people are more likely to say yes after they have received something of value. By providing something of value to others—whether it's information, support, or a favor—you may foster a sense of obligation and reciprocity, increasing the likelihood that they will reciprocate in return.

2. Social Proof: According to the social proof concept, if people see others doing something, they are more inclined to do it themselves. By offering social proof, such as testimonials, case studies, or endorsements, you may show that your ideas or recommendations have helped others, making them more persuasive and attractive to your target audience.

3. Authority: According to the concept of authority, people are more likely to follow the advice or recommendations of those they believe to be credible and knowledgeable. Positioning yourself as an authority in your profession, whether through skill, experience, or credentials, can boost your influence and persuasiveness with others.

4. Consistency: According to the principle of consistency, people are more likely to keep to their commitments and ideas after making them public. By encouraging individuals to make tiny, voluntary commitments or take incremental steps in the direction you want them to go, you can boost their chances of following through and taking greater action in the future.

5. The like principle states that people are more likely to be convinced by those they know, like, and trust. You can boost your likability and influence with your audience by developing rapport, finding common ground, and identifying areas of resemblance or shared interests.

Understanding and utilizing these persuasive principles can help you influence others, develop consensus, and achieve your business goals.

Applying the Psychology of Influence

In addition to comprehending the principles of persuasion, it is critical to comprehend the psychology of influence—the underlying variables that determine how people think, feel, and behave in response to convincing messages.

Cognitive biases are mental shortcuts or heuristics that influence our decision-making processes and perceptions of our surroundings. Understanding and using cognitive biases allows you to improve the effectiveness of your persuasive attempts and influence others.

For example, the availability heuristic implies that people make decisions based on information that is easily accessible to them. You can boost the persuasive power of your message by including vivid examples, anecdotes, or testimonials that make it more memorable and accessible.

Similarly, the anchoring effect says that people tend to make decisions based on the first piece of information they get, even if it is arbitrary or irrelevant. By framing your message in a way that stresses a specific reference point or comparison, you can affect how people perceive and assess your arguments and recommendations.

Another important idea in influence psychology is cognitive dissonance theory, which describes the discomfort that occurs when our beliefs or behaviors conflict with one another. You can boost the persuasiveness of your message and drive your audience to act by emphasizing inconsistencies or contradictions in their beliefs or actions and proposing a solution or alternative to reconcile them.

Understanding and implementing the psychology of influence can help you persuade others, develop agreement, and achieve your business goals.

Practical Strategies for Persuasion

In addition to comprehending the concepts of persuasion and the psychology of influence, it is critical to create practical tactics for effectively convincing others in the workplace. Here are some strategies to consider:

1. Understand Your Audience: Customize your persuasive efforts to meet the requirements, preferences, and expectations of your target audience. Consider their motives, worries, and priorities, then customize your message to appeal to them.

2. Establish Credibility and Trust: Demonstrate your competence, integrity, and dependability to position yourself as a reliable and trustworthy source of information. Provide evidence and examples to back up your ideas and recommendations, and communicate openly and honestly.

3. Frame Your Message Effectively: Emphasize the benefits and advantages of adopting your point of view or pursuing a specific course of action. Highlight the good results and

prospective rewards, and address any objections or concerns upfront.

4. Use persuasive language and rhetoric, such as rich imagery, potent metaphors, and emotional appeals. Create a message that provokes powerful emotions and connects with your audience on a personal level.

5. Provide social proof and endorsements.

Provide social proof, such as testimonials, case studies, or endorsements, to demonstrate the value and success of your ideas or recommendations. Demonstrate that others have benefited from your ideas and that they can rely on you to achieve outcomes.

Applying these practical persuasive methods will improve your capacity to influence others, develop consensus, and achieve your business objectives.

Ethical Considerations for Persuasion

Finally, evaluate the ethical aspects of persuasion and make sure your persuasive efforts are carried out with integrity, honesty, and respect for others.

First and foremost, be upfront and honest in your communication, and avoid using misleading or manipulative strategies to influence others. Present your arguments and recommendations truthfully and transparently, with evidence and examples to back up your views.

Second, it is critical to respect others' autonomy and free will and avoid coercing or pushing them to take a specific course of action. Instead, concentrate on presenting compelling arguments and offering information and tools that will enable others to make educated judgments based on their interests and values.

Finally, assess the potential repercussions of your persuasion attempts and ensure that they are consistent with ethical ideas and values. Ask yourself if your persuasive methods are fair, polite, and conducive to beneficial outcomes for all parties involved, and be willing to change your strategy if needed.

By conducting your persuasive efforts with integrity, honesty, and respect for others, you can earn your audience's confidence, credibility, and goodwill while also achieving your goals ethically and sustainably.

Verdict

In this chapter, we looked at the art of persuasion, which is vital for success in business and beyond. We've covered the fundamentals of persuasion, the psychology of influence, practical tactics for convincing people, and ethical considerations. Mastering the art of persuasion and using it with integrity and honesty allows you to influence others, develop agreement, and achieve your objectives in any corporate setting. So, dear reader, I invite you to embrace the power of persuasion and maximize the effectiveness of your communication skills. The world is waiting for your message—speak with intellect, integrity, and influence, and watch as opportunities open up in front of you.

Chapter 6: Strategic Meetings: Maximum Impact

Welcome to Chapter 6 of "Speak Intelligent: Gaining Knowledge of Business Communication for Success." In this chapter, we'll look at strategic meetings, which are an important part of corporate communication that may have a big impact on organizational success. We will look at the concepts of preparing and leading strategic meetings, as well as how to engage participants and facilitate constructive discussions. We will also cover tactics for successful follow-up and action planning to ensure that discussions result in significant outcomes. Practical insights, real-world examples, and concrete methods will teach you how to maximize the impact of your meetings and create success in any work context.

Planning and Leading Strategic Meetings

Strategic meetings are more than just gatherings; they provide chances to align goals, make choices, and accelerate progress toward company goals. Meetings, on the other hand, can become ineffective and fail to fulfill their goals if they are not properly planned and led. In this section, we will talk about how to effectively arrange and lead strategic meetings.

1. Set Clear Objectives: Before scheduling a meeting, determine its purpose and objectives. What are you hoping to accomplish? Do you want to make decisions, produce ideas, or provide updates? Setting specific objectives helps to keep the meeting focused and productive.

2. Create an Agenda: Create a detailed agenda stating the topics to be covered, the time given to each item, and the anticipated goals. Share the agenda with attendees in advance so they may prepare and contribute effectively.

3. Invite the Right People: Make sure the right people are invited to the meeting—those with the necessary experience or authority to contribute to the discussion and decision-making processes. Avoid inviting people who will disrupt the meeting or waste time.

4. Choose the Right Format: Based on your meeting's objectives and participant preferences, choose the most acceptable format. Will it be an in-person meeting, a virtual conference, or a hybrid model? Select the format that best promotes involvement and cooperation.

5. Facilitate Active Participation: As the meeting's leader, you must ensure that all attendees actively participate. Encourage open dialogue by asking probing questions and inviting input from quieter members. Make sure that everyone has an opportunity to contribute their ideas and observations.

6. Respect participants' time by adhering to the agenda and managing time efficiently. Start and end the meeting on time, provide enough time for each agenda item, and use timekeeping tools to stay on track.

7. Encourage Constructive Conflict: Healthy debate and conflict resolution can result in better decision-making and innovation. Encourage varied ideas and courteous dissent, but keep debates focused and productive.

8. Document critical decisions, action items, and next steps as they arise during the meeting. Assign roles and timelines to guarantee accountability and follow-through once the meeting is over.

By adhering to these strategic meeting planning and leadership principles, you can ensure that your meetings are focused, productive, and in line with company objectives.

Engaging participants and facilitating productive discussions.

Effective meetings require engaging participants and facilitating constructive discussions. Here are some techniques that encourage involvement and collaboration:

1. Establish a Positive setting: Set the tone for the meeting by providing a welcoming and inclusive setting in which all attendees feel appreciated and respected. Begin with a brief icebreaker or introduction to let people feel comfortable and connected.

2. Use Interactive Techniques: To stimulate involvement and creativity, try brainstorming, group exercises, or breakout sessions. Provide guests with the opportunity to actively offer their ideas and perspectives.

3. Use strong questions to encourage critical thinking and meaningful discussion. Instead of using simple yes or no answers, ask open-ended questions that stimulate contemplation and exploration.

4. Actively listen to individuals' remarks and demonstrate genuine interest in their ideas and perspectives. Empathic listening involves respecting their sentiments and accepting their experiences.

5. Manage dominating Personalities: Be aware of dominating personalities who may dominate a conversation or silence quieter

members. Encourage balanced involvement by seeking comments from all attendees and intervening when needed to ensure everyone has an opportunity to speak.

6. Provide feedback and validation to participants to recognize their contributions and encourage future engagement. Recognize great discoveries, applaud new ideas, and emphasize the relevance of varied perspectives.

7. Facilitate Consensus-Building: Direct the debate toward consensus-building by identifying common ground and points of agreement among participants. Use facilitation strategies including summarizing essential points, highlighting areas of agreement, and soliciting feedback on outstanding issues.

8. Manage Difficult Dynamics: Use tact and diplomacy to address any problematic dynamics or disputes that occur throughout the meeting. Redirect negative energy into constructive discourse, and act as needed to keep a courteous and productive environment.

By engaging participants and encouraging fruitful discussions, you may tap into your team's collective insight and expertise to produce significant solutions in meetings.

Strategies for Following Up and Action Planning

What occurs following a conference usually determines its genuine impact. Effective follow-up and action planning are critical for turning meeting discussions into actual results and accelerating progress toward corporate objectives. Here are some follow-up tactics and action plans:

1. Summarize main Decisions and Action Items: Following the meeting, distribute a summary of the main decisions, action items, and future steps. Ensure that all participants are aware of their roles and deadlines moving ahead.

2. Assign Ownership and Accountability: Assign each action item to a specific individual or team, and set timeframes for completion.

Establish accountability tools to track progress and ensure commitments are met.

3. Provide Resources and help: Give participants the tools and help them need to complete their action plans successfully. Provide direction, help, and access to necessary information or resources to aid implementation.

4. Provide Regular Updates: Keep participants informed of progress on action items by giving regular updates and status reports. Communicate any issues or impediments that may develop, and work with stakeholders to identify solutions.

5. Celebrate Successes and Milestones: Recognize accomplishments and milestones reached as a result of accomplishing goals. Recognize and recognize people or teams for their contributions and accomplishments, promoting a culture of accountability and quality.

6. Evaluate Meeting Effectiveness: Conduct periodic reviews to determine meeting effectiveness and identify areas for

improvement. Solicit comments from participants on what worked well and what may be improved for future meetings.

7. Adjust and Iterate: Use evaluation feedback and insights to continuously adjust and iterate on meeting methods and practices. Experiment with new tactics, strategies, or formats to increase meeting effectiveness and engagement.

8. Align with Organizational Goals: Ensure that meeting outcomes and action plans are consistent with the overall organizational goals and strategic priorities. Connect meeting topics and conclusions to key performance indicators and desired business results.

Implementing these follow-up and action-planning tactics can ensure that your meetings produce meaningful results and drive progress toward organizational success.

Verdict

In this chapter, we looked at the art of strategic meetings, which are an important part of business communication that may have a big impact on organizational success. We've covered the fundamentals of organizing and leading strategic meetings, engaging participants, and facilitating fruitful discussions. We've also addressed tactics for good follow-up and action planning to ensure that meetings produce significant results. Mastering the art of strategic meetings allows you to optimize the impact of your

Meetings drive success in any company context. So, dear reader, I welcome you to use these ideas and tactics in your meetings, and watch as you accomplish real results and make progress toward your organization's goals. Speak intelligently, clearly, and impactful, and let your meetings serve as catalysts for positive change and innovation.

Chapter 7: Strategic Presentations for Captivating Audiences

Welcome to Chapter 7 of "Speak Intelligent: Gaining Knowledge of Business Communication for Success." In this chapter, we'll take a look at strategic presentations, which are essential skills for professionals in any industry. Whether you're proposing a new concept, providing a project update, or delivering a keynote address, the ability to captivate your audience and successfully transmit your message is critical to success. Here, we'll look at how to prepare engaging and persuasive presentations, deliver them with confidence and authority, and enhance visual aids for optimum impact. Practical insights, real-world examples, and actionable tactics can help you improve your presentation skills and create a lasting impact on your audience.

Creating Engaging and Persuasive Presentations

Thorough preparation is essential for a good presentation. Here are some important steps for creating compelling and persuasive presentations:

1. Know Your Audience: Understand who your audience is, what they care about, and what they hope to get out of your presentation. Personalize your content and messaging to reflect their interests, issues, and preferences.

2. Clarify Your Objectives: Define the goals of your presentation—what do you want to accomplish? Do you want to inform, convince, or inspire your audience? Clearly define your objectives to guide the creation of your content and structure.

3. Create a fascinating Narrative: Build your presentation around a fascinating narrative with a defined beginning, middle, and end. Begin with a great beginning that captures your audience's attention, followed by a well-organized body that cohesively conveys your important points, and finish with a memorable

closure that reinforces your message and calls for action.

4. Concentrate on Key statements: Condense your information into brief, memorable key statements that connect with your audience and support your goals. Keep your material focused and relevant, and avoid using jargon or technical details that could overwhelm or confuse your audience.

5. Use Visual Aids Effectively: Visual aids such as presentations, charts, graphs, and movies can help you illustrate crucial concepts and engage your audience visually. Choose clear, captivating, and relevant pictures for your message, and use them sparingly to supplement—not overwhelm—your spoken words.

6. Practice, Practice, and Practice: Rehearse your presentation several times to ensure that it is delivered smoothly and with confidence. Practice speaking clearly and confidently, pacing your speech appropriately, and incorporating gestures and body language to enhance your message.

7. Anticipate Questions and Objections: Prepare intelligent responses ahead of time in case your audience has any questions or concerns. Proactively addressing complaints indicates preparation and credibility, as well as helping to create trust with your audience.

Following these steps will allow you to create compelling and persuasive presentations that will connect with your audience and effectively achieve your goals.

Deliver with Confidence and Authority

Confidence and authority are crucial attributes for making captivating presentations. Here are some suggestions to help you radiate confidence and authority while presenting:

1. Project Confidence: Stand tall, make eye contact, and speak clearly and convincingly. Projecting confidence through your demeanor, tone of voice, and body language can instill trust and trustworthiness in your audience.

2. Speak with Authority: Speak with authority and conviction, providing a sense of expertise

and knowledge about your subject. Use confident words and strong remarks to command attention and deliver your message authoritatively.

3. Engage Your Audience: Encourage audience participation in your presentation by including interactive components such as questions, polls, or group activities. Encourage participation and comments to ensure a lively and interactive presentation experience.

4. be honest and authentic in your speech, demonstrating passion and love for your subject. Authenticity fosters rapport and connection with your target audience, making your message more appealing and memorable.

5. Manage Nervousness: Deep breathing, visualization, or positive self-talk can all be used to help you relax and reduce your anxiety. Turn your apprehensive energy into enthusiasm and passion for your topic, and use it to power your presentation delivery.

6. Adapt to Feedback: Be open to receiving feedback and adjusting your presentation style based on audience reactions. Pay attention to

signs like body language, facial expressions, and verbal feedback, and adapt your delivery accordingly to keep your audience engaged and interested.

7. Maintain professionalism and calmness during your presentation, especially if faced with unanticipated problems or technical issues. Maintain your composure, flexibility, and adaptability, exhibiting your ability to bear pressure gracefully and confidently.

You may fascinate your audience and leave a lasting impact on them by exuding confidence and authority during your presentation performance.

Enhancing Visual Aids for Maximum Impact.

Visual aids are essential for increasing the effectiveness of presentations. Here are some techniques for increasing the effect of your visual aids:

1. Keep it Simple: Visual aids should be simple and uncomplicated, with a focus on

communicating important messages and supporting your narrative. Avoid cluttering slides with too much text or graphics, as this might overwhelm your audience and distract from your point.

2. Use High-Quality Graphics: Use high-quality graphics, photos, and videos to make your presentation more visually appealing. Choose graphics that are relevant, professional, and visually appealing, as well as clear, sharp, and understandable.

3. Follow Design Best Practices: When producing visual aids, use consistent fonts, colors, and layouts across your presentation. Use contrast to emphasize key information, and use white space to promote reading and visual clarity.

4. Convey a Story with Data: Use charts, graphs, and info graphics to convey a story about data and statistics. Visualizing data can assist your audience grasp complex information, hence reinforcing your main messages and insights.

5. Use multimedia components like as films, animations, or audio clips to bring diversity and interest to your presentation. Multimedia can help break up the monotony of slides while keeping your audience engaged and attentive.

6. Practice Visual Consistency: Ensure that all visual aids are consistent with your branding guidelines and presentation theme. Consistent visuals give your brand a cohesive and professional look and feel, reinforcing its identity and message.

7. Use Visuals to Improve Understanding: Strategically use visual aids to help students understand and remember key concepts. Break down complex ideas into digestible visual components and use visuals to demonstrate relationships, comparisons, or processes clearly and intuitively.

By incorporating these strategies into your visual aids, you can create compelling and memorable presentations that connect with your audience and leave a lasting impression.

Verdict

In this chapter, we looked at the art of strategic presentation, which is an essential skill for professionals in any field. We've talked about the importance of preparing engaging and persuasive presentations, speaking with confidence and authority, and improving visual aids for maximum impact. Mastering and effectively applying these skills will allow you to captivate your audience, convey your message with clarity and conviction, and achieve your objectives in any presentation setting. So, dear reader, I invite you to incorporate these insights and strategies into your presentations and watch as you captivate your audience and leave a lasting impression that drives success in your personal and professional endeavors. Speak with intelligence, clarity, and impact, and let your presentations serve as catalysts for positive change and influence in the world.

Chapter 8: Strategic Networking: Establishing Meaningful Connections

Welcome to Chapter 8 of "Speak Intelligent: Gaining Knowledge of Business Communication for Success." In this chapter, we'll look at the art of strategic networking, which is essential for making meaningful connections, cultivating relationships, and driving business success. Networking is more than just exchanging business cards or connecting on social media; it's about cultivating genuine relationships, capitalizing on opportunities, and building a network of support and resources to help you advance in your career. We'll look at the principles of developing and maintaining professional relationships, utilizing networking events and platforms, and cultivating a strategic network for success. Through practical insights, real-world examples, and actionable strategies, you will learn how to use networking to advance your career and achieve your objectives.

Developing and nurturing professional relationships

At its core, networking is about establishing and nurturing mutually beneficial professional relationships based on trust and respect. Here are some important ideas for developing and maintaining professional relationships:

1. Be Genuine and Authentic: Authenticity is key for networking. Be authentic, truthful, and transparent in your dealings with others. Show genuine interest in getting to know them as people, rather than just possible contacts or leads.

2. Listen more than you talk: Active listening is essential for effective networking. Take the time to listen attentively to others, ask thoughtful questions, and show genuine interest in their experiences, challenges, and goals. Listening attentively creates rapport and exhibits respect for other's viewpoints.

3. Offer Value and assistance: Be generous with your time, knowledge, and resources, and look for opportunities to offer value and assistance to others. Whether it's providing

advice, making introductions, or sharing resources, offering value develops goodwill and improves connections.

4. Follow Through on Commitments: Honor your commitments and follow through on pledges made during networking contacts. Whether it's sending an email, making an introduction, or following up on a discussion, exhibiting reliability and responsibility develops confidence and credibility.

5. Stay Connected and Engaged: Stay connected and engaged with your network frequently. Keep in touch by email, phone conversations, or social media, and attempt to attend networking events and industry gatherings. Consistent communication helps sustain and improve relationships over time.

6. Be Proactive in searching for Opportunities: Take a proactive attitude to networking by searching out opportunities to interact with others and extend your network. Attend networking events, join professional groups, and participate in online communities about your field or industry.

7. Be Patient and Persistent: Building genuine relationships takes time and effort, so be patient and persistent in your networking activities. Don't anticipate rapid results or instant gratification—instead, focus on maintaining relationships over the long term and cultivating true connections.

By adopting these principles, you may develop and cultivate professional connections that are founded on trust, respect, and mutual support, laying the foundation for networking success.

Leveraging Networking Events and Platforms

Networking events and platforms provide great opportunities to engage with people, exchange ideas, and develop your professional network. Here are some techniques for exploiting networking events and platforms effectively:

1. Create Clear Goals: Before attending a networking event or joining a networking site, create clear goals for what you intend to

achieve. Are you wanting to build new connections, learn about industry trends, or explore potential opportunities? Having defined goals helps focus your efforts and optimize your influence.

2. Prepare Elevator Pitch: Prepare a succinct and convincing elevator pitch that highlights your talents, experience, and goals. Your elevator pitch should be quick, memorable, and suited to the audience and context of the networking event or platform.

3. Initiate talks: Take the initiative to strike up talks with individuals at networking events or online platforms. Approach people in a warm manner, introduce yourself, and ask open-ended questions to start a meaningful conversation.

4. Listen and Learn: Actively listen to others and strive to learn from their experiences, thoughts, and viewpoints. To gain a better understanding and rapport with other networkers, be curious and ask intelligent questions.

5. Exchange Contact Information: Share your contact information with folks you meet at networking events or online platforms. Connect on professional networking sites like LinkedIn and send a personalized message to show your interest in staying in touch.

6. Follow-Up after Events: After networking events, follow up with new connections to strengthen your relationship and continue the discussion. Send a tailored email or message thanking them for the opportunity to connect and expressing your desire to explore potential synergies or collaborations.

7. Reciprocal networking is a two-way street, so take the initiative to offer support and assistance to people in your network. Make introductions, suggest people, and offer assistance wherever possible to demonstrate your worth as a trustworthy and reliable source.

By properly utilizing networking events and platforms, you can broaden your professional network, make new connections, and discover important chances for collaboration and advancement.

Building a Strategic Network for Success.

Building a strategic network entails developing relationships with people who can offer you support, direction, and chances to help you achieve your objectives. Here are some strategies for building a strategic network for success:

1. Identify Key Contacts: Identify key contacts in your sector or field who have experience, influence, or connections that are relevant to your aims. Mentors, advisors, industry experts, and peers can all provide useful insights and support.

2. Diversify Your Network: Connect with people from various backgrounds, sectors, and opinions. Seek out relationships with other perspectives, abilities, and experiences to improve your network and broaden your horizons.

3. Invest in Relationships: Invest time and effort in establishing relationships with critical people in your network. Be proactive in reaching out, staying in touch, and providing

support, and show real concern for their well-being and success.

4. Attend industry events, conferences, and seminars to connect with other professionals and thought leaders in your sector. These events offer important opportunities to network with influencers, exchange ideas, and remain current on industry trends and advancements.

5. Join professional organizations, associations, or networking groups based on your industry or hobbies. Participate actively in meetings, activities, and committees to foster relationships, share expertise, and give back to your profession or community.

6. Seek Mentorship and Guidance: Look for experienced experts or leaders in your industry who can offer useful advice, feedback, and support. Establishing mentorship relationships can help you grow personally and professionally while also providing vital insights and direction along your career path.

7. Give Back to Your Network: You can help others in your network by providing them with

support, direction, and assistance. Share your knowledge and skills, make introductions, and offer possibilities for growth and development to improve your relationships and foster goodwill.

By developing a strategic network of relationships based on trust, respect, and mutual support, you can gain access to valuable resources, opportunities, and insights that will help you advance your career and achieve your objectives.

Verdict

In this chapter, we've looked at the art of strategic networking, which is essential for making meaningful connections, cultivating relationships, and driving commercial success. We've covered the fundamentals of developing and maintaining professional relationships, utilizing networking events and platforms, and constructing a strategic network for success. Applying these concepts and tactics will help you extend your professional network, make new connections, and

Discover tremendous prospects for collaboration and growth. So, dear reader, I invite you to embrace the power of networking and leverage your relationships to develop your career and achieve your objectives. Speak with knowledge, clarity, and impact, and allow your network to be a source of encouragement, inspiration, and success in your personal and professional lives.

Chapter 9: Cultural Intelligence and Business Communication

Welcome to Chapter 9 of "Speak Intelligent: Gaining Knowledge of Business Communication for Success." This chapter discusses the crucial role of cultural intelligence in business communication. In today's globalized world, good cross-cultural communication is critical for developing strong relationships, encouraging cooperation, and driving success in varied corporate situations. Here, we'll look at the fundamentals of understanding cultural differences in communication, adjusting communication methods across cultures, and developing cross-cultural competency for success. Through practical insights, real-world examples, and actionable tactics, you will learn how to confidently manage cultural complexity and communicate effectively in every cultural setting.

Understanding Cultural Differences in Communication

Culture influences how people communicate, perceive information, and connect with others. Understanding cultural differences is critical for navigating varied business environments and establishing meaningful relationships with colleagues, clients, and partners from all over the world. Here are some important ideas for understanding cultural differences in communication:

1. Cultural Dimensions: Learn about individualism vs. collectivism, high-context vs. low-context communication, and power distance. These factors offer useful insights into cultural values, customs, and communication styles from other civilizations.

2. Nonverbal Communication: Understand the significance of nonverbal communication cues including body language, facial expressions, and gestures in transmitting meaning across cultures. Be aware of cultural differences in nonverbal communication and adjust your nonverbal behaviors properly to avoid misunderstandings.

3. Language and Linguistic Diversity: Recognize the linguistic diversity that exists in global corporate environments, and be attentive to language barriers and differences in language skills. Use plain and simple English, avoid slang or colloquial terms, and be patient and flexible while talking with non-native speakers.

4. Understand the cultural values, norms, and social conventions that exist in diverse civilizations. Be mindful of cultural taboos, sensitivities, and preferences surrounding themes such as hierarchy, authority, gender roles, and personal space.

5. Recognize that communication styles differ amongst cultures, with some prioritizing direct and clear communication and others preferring indirect and implicit communication. Adjust your communication style to reflect cultural norms and expectations, and be adaptable in your approach.

6. Listening and Empathy: When speaking with people from other cultures, engage in active listening and empathy. Seek to grasp their ideas, experiences, and cultural context, and

show tolerance and openness to opposing viewpoints.

7. Avoiding preconceptions: Avoid preconceptions and generalizations about cultural groups, acknowledging that people within a culture may differ in communication styles, tastes, and actions. Treat everyone as an individual, and avoid making conclusions based on cultural stereotypes.

Understanding cultural communication variations and treating cross-cultural encounters with sensitivity and knowledge can help you develop trust, foster understanding, and effectively traverse cultural complexity in the workplace.

Adapting Communication Styles across Cultures

Adapting communication techniques across cultures necessitates adaptability, empathy, and cultural understanding. Here are some techniques for adjusting your communication style to effectively communicate with people from various cultural backgrounds:

1. Be Observant and Attentive: Notice cultural cues and nuances in communication, such as tone of voice, body language, and conversational patterns. Be aware of your audience's cultural context and preferences, and change your communication approach accordingly.

2. Flexibility and Openness: Be adaptable and open-minded in your approach to communication, acknowledging that different cultures may have distinct communication techniques and standards. Adapt your communication style to meet multiple preferences and expectations, and be prepared to try new techniques to establish common ground.

3. Clarify and Confirm Understanding: Avoid misconceptions and misinterpretations by clarifying and confirming understanding during cross-cultural contact. Use paraphrase, summarizing, and clarifying questions to ensure that your message is received and understood correctly by your audience.

4. Respect Cultural Norms: Follow cultural norms and practices about communication, hierarchy, and social decorum. Be aware of cultural sensitivities and avoid acts or language that could be interpreted as rude or objectionable in a certain cultural environment.

5. Seek Feedback and Guidance: Consult with people who are knowledgeable about your target audience's cultural peculiarities. Solicit feedback from coworkers, mentors, or cultural consultants who can provide useful insights and recommendations on how to effectively change your communication style.

6. Focus on developing rapport and trust with people from various cultural backgrounds by exhibiting respect, understanding, and genuine interest in their points of view. Building trust is vital for efficient cross-cultural communication and collaboration.

7. Practice Cultural Empathy: Put yourself in the shoes of others and try to comprehend their cultural perspective, beliefs, and experiences. Approach cross-cultural

relationships with curiosity and humility, and be willing to learn from other cultures' ideas.

By tailoring your communication style to your audience's cultural norms and preferences, you may create cross-cultural trust, understanding, and collaboration, resulting in more effective communication and stronger connections.

Developing Cross-cultural Competence for Success

Developing cross-cultural competency is critical for success in today's international business climate. Here are some techniques for improving your cross-cultural competence:

1. Cultural Awareness and Self-Reflection: Develop your cultural awareness and self-reflection skills by investigating your own cultural identity, biases, and preconceptions. Consider how your cultural heritage affects your communication style, actions, and worldview, and work to acquire cultural humility and a willingness to learn.

2. Cultural Education and Training: Look for opportunities to further your understanding of different cultures and improve your cross-cultural competency. Attend workshops, seminars, or courses on intercultural communication, diversity, and cultural competency to broaden your knowledge and abilities.

3. Cross-Cultural Experiences: Travel, study abroad programs, or overseas assignments can expose you to new cultures and ways of thinking. Immerse yourself in a variety of locations and interact with people from different cultural backgrounds to extend your perspective and increase your understanding.

4. Build Relationships Across Cultures: Actively seek out opportunities to connect and collaborate with people from other cultural backgrounds. Expand your social and professional network by engaging in cross-cultural networking, joining multicultural teams or organizations, and attending intercultural events.

5. Seek Feedback and Learn from Mistakes: Get feedback from others on your cross-

cultural interactions and communication efforts, and be willing to learn from errors or misunderstandings. Take comments as an opportunity for growth and self-improvement, and strive to continually increase your cross-cultural competency over time.

6. Cultivate cultural adaptability and flexibility.

Navigating cross-cultural encounters and situations. Be prepared to adapt your communication style, behavior, and expectations to meet other cultural norms and preferences, and approach new cultural encounters with an open mind and eagerness to discover.

7. Encourage diversity and inclusion in the workplace by raising cultural awareness, sensitivity, and respect among colleagues and stakeholders. Create inclusive settings in which people of many cultural origins feel appreciated, respected, and empowered to share their unique ideas and abilities.

Building cross-cultural competency improves your capacity to communicate effectively, work productively, and manage cultural difficulties with confidence and sensitivity in the global business world.

Verdict

In this chapter, we discussed the crucial role of cultural intelligence in corporate communication. We've covered the fundamentals of identifying cultural differences in communication, adapting communication methods across cultures, and developing cross-cultural competency for success. By embracing cultural variety, raising cultural awareness, and polishing your cross-cultural skills, you can confidently negotiate cultural complexity and communicate successfully in any cultural situation. So, dear reader, I invite you to embrace the principles and strategies outlined in this chapter and work toward becoming a culturally intelligent communicator who bridges cultural divides, fosters understanding, and drives success in today's interconnected world. Speak with intelligence, clarity, and empathy, and let your cultural intelligence guide you as you make meaningful connections and foster cross-cultural collaboration.

Chapter 10: Strategic Feedback and Recognition.

Welcome to Chapter 10 of "Speak Intelligent: Gaining Knowledge of Business Communication for Success." In this chapter, we'll look at how strategic feedback and recognition can help foster a culture of growth, collaboration, and excellence in the workplace. Effective feedback and recognition are critical for empowering employees, improving performance, and creating a positive work environment in which people feel valued, motivated, and appreciated. Here, we'll look at how to effectively give and receive feedback, recognize and acknowledge contributions, and foster a culture of growth and appreciation. Practical insights, real-world examples, and actionable strategies will teach you how to use feedback and recognition as powerful tools for personal and organizational development.

Giving and Receiving Feedback Effectively

Feedback is an effective tool for encouraging growth, learning, and improvement in the workplace. Here are some principles for providing and receiving feedback effectively

1. Provide feedback in a timely and specific manner, ideally shortly after the observed behavior or performance. Provide specific and concrete feedback, emphasizing observable behaviors and outcomes rather than vague generalizations.

2. When providing feedback, prioritize behaviors and actions over personality traits or character judgments. Provide objective and nonjudgmental feedback, focusing on observable facts and their impact on performance or outcomes.

3. Balance Positive and Constructive Feedback: Your feedback should include both positive reinforcement and constructive criticism. Recognize strengths and successes while also offering advice and suggestions for improvement. Balance is essential for

maintaining motivation and morale while encouraging growth and development.

4. Consider using the SBI (Situation-Behavior-Impact) model to provide feedback. Describe the specific situation or behavior observed, explain its impact or consequences, and offer suggestions for improvement or change. This structured approach promotes clarity and effectiveness in feedback delivery.

5. Encourage Self-Reflection and Ownership: Encourage people to reflect on themselves and take responsibility for their development by soliciting their own opinions and thoughts. Encourage open debate and discussion, and allow everyone to share their thoughts, concerns, and suggestions for change.

6. Be Receptive to Feedback: Be open and willing to receive feedback from others, regardless of their position or status. Actively listen, express thanks for input, and endeavor to grasp other people's viewpoints and thoughts. Remember that feedback is two-way, and everyone has valuable insights to share.

7. Follow Up and Follow Through: Follow up on feedback discussions and commitments, and offer ongoing assistance and guidance as needed. Check-in periodically to check progress, offer additional support or resources, and celebrate successes along the way.

By following these principles, you can create a culture of open communication, trust, and continuous improvement where feedback is valued, constructive, and actionable.

Recognizing and Acknowledging Contributions

Recognition is a powerful motivator that can inspire loyalty, engagement, and high performance among employees. Here are some strategies for recognizing and acknowledging contributions effectively:

1. Be Genuine and Specific: Be genuine and specific in your recognition efforts, acknowledging individuals for their unique contributions and accomplishments. Highlight

specific behaviors, achievements, or outcomes that demonstrate excellence, effort, or impact.

2. Public and Private Recognition: Consider both public and private forms of recognition, based on the interests and comfort levels of individuals. Public recognition, such as shout-outs at team meetings or newsletters, can foster a sense of pride and belonging, while private recognition, such as personal notes or one-on-one meetings, can be more personal and meaningful.

3. Tailor Recognition to Preferences: Tailor recognition efforts to the preferences and preferences of individuals, taking into account their personality, communication style, and preferences for receiving feedback. Some individuals may enjoy public recognition and appreciation, while others may prefer more quiet and discreet forms of acknowledgment.

4. Foster Peer-to-Peer acknowledgment: Encourage peer-to-peer acknowledgment by establishing opportunities for colleagues to acknowledge and appreciate one another's accomplishments. Peer recognition develops a sense of camaraderie and teamwork, and

encourages individuals to recognize and appreciate the achievements of their peers.

5. Link Recognition to Values and Goals: Link recognition initiatives to organizational values, goals, and priorities to promote alignment and commitment. Recognize individuals who reflect and exemplify core values, demonstrate remarkable performance, or contribute to major company projects and objectives.

6. Be Consistent and Regular: Be consistent and regular in your recognition efforts, honoring contributions and successes in a timely and continuous manner. Regular acknowledgment helps promote great behaviors and attitudes and expresses respect for the efforts and dedication of individuals.

7. Celebrate Milestones and Achievements: Celebrate milestones, achievements, and victories as a team to promote a culture of celebration, togetherness, and achievement. Host recognition events, award ceremonies, or team outings to honor key accomplishments and milestones, and to demonstrate appreciation for the collaborative efforts of the team.

Recognizing and appreciating achievements properly may inspire and motivate employees, reinforce positive behaviors and attitudes, and promote a workplace culture of respect and recognition.

Promoting a Culture of Growth and Appreciation

A culture of growth and appreciation is distinguished by ongoing learning, development, and celebration of individual and group efforts. Here are some techniques for cultivating such a culture.

1. Promote Learning and Development: Promote a culture of continuous learning and development by offering opportunities for skill-building, training, and professional growth. Invest in staff development programs, courses, and tools that allow individuals to enhance their skills and capacities.

2. Encourage Feedback and Reflection: Encourage feedback and reflection as vital components of personal and professional

progress. Create a secure and supportive workplace where individuals feel comfortable seeking and receiving criticism, and where self-reflection and self-improvement are appreciated and encouraged.

3. Lead by Example: Lead by example by embracing the values of growth and appreciation in your actions and behaviors. Demonstrate a dedication to lifelong learning and development, and recognize and acknowledge the contributions of others openly and truly.

4. Provide progression opportunities: Allow for progression and professional growth based on merit and performance. Provide clear avenues for advancement and development, as well as support and resources to assist individuals in moving forward in their careers and achieving their goals.

5. Encourage innovation and creativity by fostering a culture of experimentation, risk-taking, and learning from failure. Celebrate innovative ideas and activities, and create a supportive climate in which people feel

encouraged to pursue new opportunities and question the status quo.

6. Promote Work-Life Balance and Well-Being: Foster a culture that recognizes and supports employees' holistic needs. Encourage flexible working arrangements, encourage mental and physical wellness initiatives, and offer resources and assistance for stress management and balance.

7. Recognize and celebrate collective achievements and successes as a team, taking into account the contributions of all individuals who contributed to the accomplishment. Emphasize the significance of cooperation, collaboration, and shared achievement in enhancing organizational performance and growth.

Fostering a culture of growth and appreciation can help you establish an atmosphere in which employees feel valued, driven, and empowered to fulfill their greatest potential, resulting in workplace success and greatness.

Verdict

In this chapter, we've looked at how strategic feedback and recognition may help build a workplace culture of growth, collaboration, and excellence. We've talked about the importance of offering and receiving criticism effectively, recognizing and celebrating accomplishments, and cultivating a culture of growth and appreciation. By using feedback and recognition as strong tools for personal and organizational development, you can empower employees, increase performance, and foster a pleasant work environment in which people feel valued, driven, and appreciated. So, dear reader, I encourage you to embrace the principles and tactics discussed in this chapter and work to create a culture of growth, appreciation, and greatness in your firm. Speak with wisdom, clarity, and empathy, and let your feedback and recognition efforts motivate and empower people to reach their full potential and create workplace success.

Conclusion: Reflecting on Your Path to Communication Mastery

As we conclude "Speak Intelligent: Gaining Knowledge of Business Communication for Success," consider the trip you've taken to master the art of communication. Throughout this book, we've looked at a variety of methods, approaches, and ideas to help you talk with intelligence, clarity, and impact in the ever-changing world of corporate communication. From grasping the necessity of good communication to navigating cultural challenges, providing and accepting feedback, and establishing a culture of growth and appreciation, you've gained vital insights and abilities for navigating modern-day communication.

Reflecting on Your Journey.

Take a minute to pause and reflect on your progress toward communication mastery. Consider the talents you've learned, the insights you've gained, and the obstacles you've faced along the road. Consider how your understanding of communication has grown and how you've used these ideas in your personal and professional life. Celebrate your accomplishments and recognize the growth and success you've made on this path.

Consider the times of clarity and insight when you discovered new tactics or viewpoints that changed your approach to communicating. Recall moments when you overcame obstacles or disappointments with tenacity and persistence. Recognize the fortitude and commitment required to consistently enhance and perfect your communication abilities, as well as the progress you've made toward mastery.

Moving Forward with Confidence and Purpose.

As you continue on your path, carry with you the confidence and purpose that comes from mastering the art of communication. With the knowledge, abilities, and insights learned from this book, you can confidently handle any communication issues that may arise in the future.

Accept the opportunity to apply what you've learned in your contacts with others, whether it's participating in strategic meetings, delivering fascinating presentations, or making significant connections through networking. Approach each communication opportunity with purpose and mindfulness, using the ideas and tactics you've learned to communicate intelligently, clearly, and effectively.

Remember that communication is more than just passing information; it is also about developing relationships, increasing understanding, and promoting good change. Whether you're speaking with coworkers, clients, or partners, try to connect truly, listen intently, and express empathy and respect.

Continue to explore chances for growth and development, understanding that mastery is a journey of continual learning and improvement. Stay interested, be open to new ideas and viewpoints, and see feedback as a driver for growth and creativity.

Above all, remember how communication can inspire, influence, and affect the world around you. As you negotiate the intricacies of today's corporate landscape, let your communication skills serve as a beacon of light, guiding you to success and fulfillment in your personal and professional activities.

Finally, I encourage you to apply the skills learned from this book as you continue on your journey to communication mastery. Reflect on your learnings, enjoy your accomplishments, and approach the challenges and possibilities that await you with confidence and purpose. Speak with wisdom, clarity, and impact, and allow your communication skills to drive success and fulfillment in all parts of your life. Thank you for joining me on this journey; may your communication journey be filled with development, learning, and limitless possibilities.

www.ingramcontent.com/pod-product-compliance
Lightning Source LLC
Chambersburg PA
CBHW071212240526
45470CB00018B/1803